In Christ, I Am...

God's Promises on Who You Are in Christ that Will Transform You from the Inside Out

Compiled by Krystal Kuehn and Violet James

MP

Maximum Potential, LLC

Think Like a Winner: How Renewing Your Mind with God's Word Empowers You to Win in Life is the perfect companion to *In Christ, I am*. It is highly recommended for an in-depth look at the power of renewing your mind.

You can download *In Christ, I am...* in AUDIO version and listen on your Kindle™ tablet, iPhone®, iPod®, and Android™. Download it at **Amazon.com** or **Audible.com** or **iTunes.**

Therefore, if anyone is in Christ, he is a new creation;
the old has gone, the new has come!

1 Corinthians 5:7

Table of Contents

V

FOREWARD

Many people struggle through life with low self-esteem, feelings of failure, and/or convinced of worthlessness as a result of a past sinful lifestyle, abusive relationships and/or hurtful and disappointing experiences. Jesus faithfully reaches out to us as savior, healer, liberator, etc. and when we repent of our sinful state and make Him the Lord of our lives, we experience the miracle of being born-again and we become a "new creation" in Christ Jesus. Consequently, we enter the glorious realm of seeing "old things passing away and all things becoming new" (II Cor. 5:17). Part of the "newness" is in coming to the realization that God sees us differently (Rom. 12:2). So we are challenged, through His word, to perceive ourselves likewise.

This book, entitled *"In Christ, I AM...,"* will help you immensely in that regard. First conceived by Krystal Kuehn and Violet James as a series of Bible study notes for their personal use, it fast became a more comprehensive collection of truths that will change your thinking and lifestyle. Motivated by a desire to be a blessing to others, these anointed and Godly sisters have willingly consented to share what the Lord has quickened to them by making this book available to you.

It is my joy and honor to both endorse and recommend the reading of this book. I encourage you to "... eat and be satisfied; that the Lord thy God may bless thee in all the work of thine hand which thou doest" (Duet. 14:29b).

Pastor Leonard Gardner
Senior Pastor
Zion Christian Church

"One special observation I made while reading your book is that it has a two pronged approach to it. Not only does it give force and encouragement to what I feel is part of the picture of a person's persona (personality), *self esteem;* your book gives a strong force and development to the most important part of a person's personality, *character!* You won't find this combination in a book very often. The one book in which these are always found is The Holy Bible, and yours follows it to the letter. I don't believe anyone who reads your book will argue against my observation."

William S. Arnott, Ph.D.

INTRODUCTION

Do you know who you are *in Christ*?

If you received Jesus Christ as your Lord and Savior, He is residing in you by His Holy Spirit. You can identify with who the Scriptures say you are in Christ. You can personalize God's promises to you— put your name in them. God is speaking to **you**. By faith you can receive all that God has for you. And, as you yield to the working of the Holy Spirit in your life you will be changed.

The same power that raised Jesus Christ from the dead is **in you**! The only way to walk in His power is to know God and the only way to know God is to know His Word. As we saturate ourselves in His Word and meditate on it, we learn of who God is and just what it means to be a child of God.

God wants us to know who we are in Christ Jesus. Only then can we walk in all the provisions He's made for us. As a Christian you don't ever have to be defeated in any area of your life. In Him you are more than a conqueror. You are an overcomer. There's nothing that you will ever face in this life that He hasn't already made provision for.

As you meditate on who you are in Christ, you will find your mind being renewed and your old ways of thinking will be replaced by the truth of God's Word. His Word has the power to transform your life. Once you truly understand who you are in Him, you will live the victorious, abundant life that Jesus died to give to you.

The following pages contain over 150 truths of who you are in Christ with corresponding Scriptures. May the power of the Living Word of God cleanse you, fill you, transform you, and set you free as you meditate on who you are in Christ Jesus. God bless you.

Krystal and Violet

I am who God says I am …I have what God says I have…
and I can do what God says I can do!

"For as the rain and snow come down from the heavens, and return
not there again, but water the earth and make it bring forth and
sprout, that it may give seed to the sower and bread to the eater, so
shall My word be that goes forth out of My mouth; it shall not return
to Me void—without producing any effect, useless—but it shall
accomplish that which I please and purpose, and it shall prosper in
the thing for which I sent it."

Isaiah 55:10-11, Amplified

WHEN I LOOKED IN THE MIRROR

One day as I looked in the mirror
I saw something I usually don't see
Something deeper, almost hidden
It was my very soul looking at me

"Tell me, what do you see when you look at me?"
I heard from the depths of my soul
"And, why don't you always like the person you see?
What is it that you believe about me?"

I pondered these questions and then realized
Many things I believed about myself might be lies
So I sought to find out what my Father would say
And I asked Him to help me see things His way

So He showed me someone very different and true
Someone who looked more like Him than I ever knew
Made in God's image, and so precious to Him
With beauty and purpose and His life within

I began to see clearly as God opened my eyes
And I started to change from the inside
Then I decided to look in the mirror once more
And this time I saw who Jesus died for

The lost and the sinner, the poor and the lame
The hurting, the angry, and all those in pain
I saw the beauty in those He loves and in me
And how He can change a life for all eternity

I saw His great love, His goodness and mercy
I saw His amazing grace that abounds towards me
Now I see how much He wants me to know that I can
Be all that in Christ He says that I am!

A

I am above only and not beneath; I am the head and not the tail

The Lord will make me the head, not the tail. If I pay attention to the commands of the LORD my God...and carefully follow them, I will always be at the top, never at the bottom. (Duet. 28:13, NIV)

I am above problems

I will lift up my eyes to the hills—where does my help come from? My help comes from the Lord, the Maker of heaven and earth. (Psalm 121-1-2) God raised me from death to life with Christ Jesus, and he has given me a place beside Christ in heaven. (Eph. 2:6, CEV) I set my mind and keep it set on what is above (the higher things), not on the things that are on the earth. (Colossians 3:2, Amp.)

I am accepted

Jesus said: those the Father has given me will come to me, and I will never reject them. (John 6:37, NLT) Everyone who calls on His name will be saved. (Romans 10:13) He made me accepted in the Beloved. (Ephesians 1:6)

I am accountable; I am responsible

I make a careful exploration of who I am and the work I have been given, and then sink myself into that. I won't be impressed with myself. I won't compare myself with others. I must take responsibility for doing the creative best I can with my own life. (Galatians 6:4-5, Msg)

I am anointed

I have an anointing from the Holy One, and I know all things. (1 John 2:20) The anointing I received from Him abides in me. Christ's anointing teaches me the truth on everything I need to know about myself and Him (uncontaminated by a single lie). (1 John 2:27, Msg)

I am armed
> *See also* - **I am a prayer warrior**

For though I live in the world, I do not wage war as the world does. The weapons I fight with are not the weapons of the world. On the contrary, they have divine power to demolish strongholds. I demolish arguments and every pretension that sets itself up against the knowledge of God, and I take captive every thought to make it obedient to Christ. (2 Cor. 10:3-5)   I put on the full armor of God, so that I can take my stand against the devil's schemes. For my struggle is not against flesh and blood, but against the rulers, against the authorities, against the powers of this dark world and against the spiritual forces of evil in the heavenly realms. Therefore I put on the full armor of God, so that when the day of evil comes, I may be able to stand my ground, and after I have done everything, to stand. I stand firm then, with the belt of truth buckled around my waist, with the breastplate of righteousness in place, and with my feet fitted with the readiness that comes from the gospel of peace. In addition to all this, I take up the shield of faith, with which I can extinguish all the flaming arrows of the evil one. I take the helmet of salvation and the sword of the Spirit, which is the word of God. And pray in the Spirit on all occasions with all kinds of prayers and requests. With this in mind, I will be alert and always keep on praying for all the Lord's people. (Eph. 6:11-18, NIV)

B

I am beautiful

What matters is not my outer appearance—the styling of my hair, the jewelry I wear, the cut of my clothes—but my inner disposition. I cultivate inner beauty, the gentle, gracious kind that God delights in. (1 Peter 3:3-4)

I am a believer
> *See also* - **I am saved**

It's impossible to please God apart from faith. And why? Because anyone who wants to approach God must believe both that he exists *and* that he cares enough to respond to those who seek him. (Heb. 11:6, Msg) "'If you can'?" said Jesus. "Everything is possible for one who believes." (Mark 9:23, NIV) Jesus answered and said to them, "Have faith in God. For assuredly, I say to you, whoever says to this mountain, 'Be removed and be cast into the sea,' and does not doubt in his heart, but believes that those things he says will be done, he will have whatever he says. Therefore I say to you, whatever things you ask when you pray, believe that you receive *them,* and you will have *them.* And whenever you stand praying, if you have anything against anyone, forgive him that your Father in heaven may also forgive you your trespasses. (Mark 11:23-24)

I am blessed
> *See also* - **I am favored**

Wherever I go and whatever I do, I will be blessed. (Deut. 28:6, NLT) The Lord blesses me and with favor He surrounds me as with a shield. (Psalm 5:12) I am blessed with every spiritual blessing in the heavenly places in Christ. (Ephesians 1:3). The LORD blesses me and protects me. The LORD smiles on me and is gracious to me. The LORD shows me his favor and gives me his peace. (Numbers 6:24-26, NLT)

I am bold

Jesus can sympathize with my weaknesses. He was tempted in all points as I am, yet without sin. Therefore I come boldly to the throne of grace to obtain mercy and grace to help me when I need it. (Hebrews 4:15-16) Because of Christ and my faith in him, I can now come boldly and confidently into God's presence. (Eph. 3:12, NLT) The wicked run away when no one is chasing them, but the godly are as bold as lions. (Proverbs 28:1, NLT)

I am building my spiritual house

Jesus said... "Therefore everyone who hears these words of mine and puts them into practice is like a wise man who built his house on the rock." (Matt. 7:24, NIV) Paul said... "For we are God's fellow workers; you are God's field, you are God's building. According to the grace of God which was given to me, as a wise master builder I have laid the foundation, and another builds on it. But let each one take heed how he builds on it. For no other foundation can anyone lay than that which is laid, which is Jesus Christ." (1 Corinthians 3:9-11) By wisdom a house is built, and through understanding it is established; through knowledge its rooms are filled with rare and beautiful treasures. (Proverbs 24:3-4, NIV) Unless the LORD builds the house, the builders labor in vain. Unless the LORD watches over the city, the guards stand watch in vain. (Psalm 127:1, NIV)

C

I am called

He saved me and called me with a holy calling, not according to my works, but according to His own purpose and grace which was given to me in Christ Jesus before time began. (2 Timothy 1:9)

I am carefree; I am anxious for nothing

Lord, when doubt fills my mind, when my heart is in turmoil, quiet me and give me renewed hope and cheer. (Psalm 94:19, TLB) I cast the whole of my care (all my anxieties, all my worries, all my concerns, once and for all) on You, for You care for me affectionately and care about me watchfully. (1 Peter 5:7, Amplified) I don't worry about anything, but I pray about everything. With a thankful heart I offer up my prayers and requests to God, and the peace of God which surpasses all understanding, guards my heart and mind through Christ Jesus. (Phil. 4:6-7, CEV, NKJV)

I am careful of what I say

If I want to enjoy life and see many happy days, I must keep my tongue from speaking evil and my lips from telling lies. I turn away from evil and do good. I search for peace, and work to maintain it. (1 Peter 3:10-11, NLT) Let the words of my mouth and the meditations of my heart be acceptable in your sight, O Lord, my strength and My Redeemer. (Psalm 19:14)

I am a child of God; I am a joint heir

In Christ Jesus I am a child of God through faith, for I who was baptized into Christ have clothed myself with Christ. There is neither Jew nor Gentile, neither slave nor free, nor is there male and female, for we are all one in Christ Jesus. Because I belong to Christ, I am Abraham's seed, and an heir according to the promise. (Galatians 3:26-29, NIV) Because I am his child, God has sent the Spirit of his Son into my heart, prompting me to call out, "Abba, Father." Now I am no longer a slave but God's own child. And since I am his child, God has made me his heir. (Gal. 4:6-7, NLT) And He raised me up together with Him and made me sit down together [giving me joint seating with Him] in the heavenly sphere [by virtue of my being] in Christ Jesus (the Messiah, the Anointed One). (Ephesians 2:6, Amp.)

I am chosen

I am chosen by God, chosen for the high calling of priestly work, chosen to be a holy people, God's instrument to do his work and speak out for him… to proclaim the praises of Him who called me out of darkness into His marvelous light. (1 Peter 2:9-10, Msg, NKJV) You chose me and appointed me to go and bear fruit, and that my fruit should remain, that whatever I ask the Father in Jesus' name He may give me. (John 15:16)

I am Christ-like

But I, with an unveiled face, beholding as in a mirror the glory of the Lord, am being transformed into the same image from glory to glory, just as by the Spirit of the Lord. (2 Cor. 3:18) People insulted Christ, but he did not insult them in return. Christ suffered, but he did not threaten. He let God, the One who judges rightly, take care of him. (1 Peter 2:21-23, NCV)

6

I am clean; I am pure in heart

I walk in the light as He is in the light, having fellowship with others and the blood of Jesus Christ cleanses me from all sin. If I say that I have no sin, I deceive myself, and the truth is not in me. If I confess my sins, He is faithful and just to forgive me my sins and to cleanse me from all unrighteousness. (1 John 1:7-9) Purge me with hyssop, and I shall be clean; wash me, and I shall be whiter than snow. (Psalm 51:7) Create in me a clean heart, O God, and renew a steadfast spirit within me. (Psalm 51:10)

I am comforted

Jesus said... I will not leave you comfortless; I will come to you. (John 14:18, KJV) Blessed are those who mourn, for they shall be comforted. (Matthew 5:4) In the multitude of my thoughts within me Thy comforts delight my soul. (Ps. 94:19, KJV) Now may my Lord Jesus Christ himself and God my Father...comfort me and strengthen me in every good thing I do and say. (2Thes. 2:16-17, NLT)

I am comforting others

God is my merciful Father and the source of all comfort. He comforts me in all my troubles so that I can comfort others. When they are troubled, I will be able to give them the same comfort God has given me. For the more I suffer for Christ, the more God will shower me with his comfort through Christ. (2 Cor. 1:3-5, NLT) Through the patience and comfort of the Scripture I have hope and may God grant me to be like-minded toward others. (Romans 15:4-5)

I am compassionate; I am caring; I am empathetic

When He (Jesus) saw the multitudes, He was moved with compassion for them, because they were weary and scattered, like sheep having no shepherd. (Matt. 9:36) God loved me and chose me for his own. So then, I must clothe myself with compassion, kindness, humility, gentleness, and patience. (Col. 3:12, GNT)

I am confident

For the Lord will be my confidence and will keep my foot from being caught. (Proverbs 3:26) It is better to trust in the Lord than to put confidence in man. (Psalm 118:8) Now all glory to God, who is able, through his mighty power at work within me, to accomplish infinitely more than I might ask or think. (Eph. 3:20, NLT) I can do all things through Christ who strengthens me. (Phil. 4:13) God began doing a good work in me, and...he will continue it until it is finished when Jesus Christ comes again. (Phil. 1:6, NCV) Now this is the confidence I have in Him, that if I ask anything according to His will, He hears me. (1 John 5:14)

I am content; I am satisfied
> *See also* – I am fulfilled; I am complete

I enjoy my work and accept my lot in life—it is a gift from God. I don't need to look back with sorrow on my past, for God gives me joy. (Eccel. 5:19b-20, TLB)   I am sure to do my very best and therefore, will have the personal satisfaction of work well done, and I won't need to compare myself with someone else. (Gal. 6:4, TLB)

I am courageous
> *See also* – **I am strong, I am fearless**

I am strong and of good courage; I am not afraid or dismayed, for the Lord my God is with me wherever I go. (Joshua 1:9) Hezekiah... gave them encouragement, saying, "Be strong and courageous; do not be afraid nor dismayed before the king of Assyria, nor before all the multitude that is with him; for there are more with us than with him. (2 Chron. 32:7) I will be of good courage, and He shall strengthen my heart, I hope in the LORD. (Psalm 31:24)

I am created; I am made in God's image
> *See also* – **I am special, I am a child of God**

So God created mankind in his own image, in the image of God he created them; male and female he created them. (Genesis 1:27, NIV) For You formed my inward parts; You covered me in my mother's womb. I will praise You, for I am fearfully and wonderfully made. (Psalm 139:13-14) You are my Creator. I was in Your care even before I was born. (Is. 44:2a, CEV)

I am creative

In the beginning God created....(Genesis 1:1). By faith I understand that the worlds were framed by the Word of God, so that the things which are seen were not made of things which are visible. (Heb. 11:3)

D

I am dead to sin; I am risen

For sin does not have dominion over me. I am not under the law but I'm under grace. (Rom. 6:14) God is so rich in mercy, and he loved me so much, that even though I was dead because of my sins, he gave me life when he raised Christ from the dead. (It is only by God's grace that I have been saved!) For he raised me from the dead along with Christ and seated me with him in the heavenly realms because I am united with Christ Jesus. (Eph. 2:4-6, NLT)

I am debt-free
> *See also* – **I am a tither, I am wealthy**

The LORD will open the storehouses of the skies where he keeps the rain, and he will send rain on my land at just the right times. He will make me successful in everything I do. I will have plenty of money to lend to other nations, but I won't need to borrow any myself. (Deut. 28:12, CEV) I keep out of debt and owe no man anything, except to love one another. By loving my neighbor I fulfill the Law. (Rom. 13:8, Amplified)

I am devoted; I am dedicated

No one can serve two masters. Either you will hate the one and love the other, or you will be devoted to the one and despise the other. You cannot serve both God and money. (Matthew 6:24, NIV) I shall love the Lord my God with all my heart, with all my soul, and with all my strength. (Deut. 6:5) In the morning You hear my voice, O Lord; in the morning I prepare (a prayer, a sacrifice) for You and watch and wait (for You to speak to my heart). (Psalm 5:3, Amp.)

I am diligent

I am diligent to present myself approved to God, a worker who does not need to be ashamed, rightly dividing the word of truth. (2 Timothy 2:15) I keep my heart with all diligence, for out of it spring the issues of life. (Prov. 4:23) The soul of a lazy man desires, and has nothing; But the soul of the diligent shall be made rich. (Proverbs 13:4)

I am a disciple of Christ; I am living for Christ

Christ gives meaning to my life (Christ is my life). (Col. 3:4a, CEV) My old self has been crucified with Christ. It is no longer I who live, but Christ lives in me. So I live in this earthly body by trusting in the Son of God, who loved me and gave himself for me. (Gal. 2:20, NLT) But whatever were gains to me I now consider loss for the sake of Christ. What is more, I consider everything a loss because of the surpassing worth of knowing Christ Jesus my Lord, for whose sake I have lost all things. I consider them garbage, that I may gain Christ. (Phil. 3:7-8, NIV)

I am a doer of the Word

I hear the words of Jesus and put them into practice. My house is built on the rock. (Matt. 7:24-25, NIV) I do not grow weary in doing good. (2 Thess. 3:13) I don't just listen to God's word. I must do what it says. Otherwise, I am only fooling myself. For if I listen to the word and don't obey, it is like glancing at my face in a mirror. I see myself, walk away, and forget what I look like. But if I look carefully into the perfect law that sets me free, and if I do what it says and don't forget what I heard, then God will bless me for doing it. (James 1:22-25, NLT)

E

I am empowered

You (God) are able to do exceedingly abundantly above all that I ask or think, according to the power that works in me. (Eph. 3:20-21) You have given me the keys to the kingdom of heaven, and whatever I bind on earth will be bound in heaven, and whatever I loose on earth will be loosed in heaven. (Matt. 16:19)

I am encouraged; I am edified

I am completely discouraged...Revive me by Your Word...I weep with grief; my heart is heavy with sorrow; encourage and cheer me with Your Words. (Ps. 119:25, 28, TLB) I keep my eyes on Jesus who leads me and makes my faith complete. I think of what Jesus endured...then I won't get discouraged and give up. (Heb. 12:2-3, CEV) And David was greatly distressed; for the people spake of stoning him, because the soul of all the people was grieved, every man for his sons and for his daughters: but David encouraged himself in the LORD his God. (1 Samuel 30:6, KJV) Weeping may endure for the night, but joy comes in the morning. (Ps. 30:5b)

I am encouraging others

I pursue the things which make for peace and the things by which I may edify others. (Rom. 14:19) The Lord God has given me His words of wisdom so that I may know what I should say to all these weary ones. Morning by morning He wakens me and opens my understanding to His will. (Is. 50:4, TLB)

I am equipped; I am prepared; I am capable; I am able

The God of peace...equips me with all I need to do His will. He produces in me, through the power of Jesus Christ, all that is pleasing to Him....(Heb. 13:20-21, NLT) I can do all things through Christ who strengthens me. (Phil. 4:13) You are the vine, I am the branch. I abide in You and You in me, and bear much fruit; for without You I can do nothing. (John 15:5)

I am eternal

For God so loved the world that He gave His only begotten Son; I believe in Him and I will not perish but have everlasting life. (John 3:16) And this is the testimony: that God has given me eternal life, and this life is in His Son. He who has the Son has life; he who does not have the Son of God does not have life. These things (John) has written to me who believes in the name of the Son of God, that I may know that I have eternal life, and that I may continue to believe in the name of the Son of God. (1 John 5:11-13) For the wages of sin is death, but the gift of God is eternal life in Christ Jesus my Lord. (Romans 6:23)

I am an example
> *See also* – I am the light of the world, I am Christ-like

I am a letter, written on hearts, known and read by everyone. ...written not with ink but with the Spirit of the living God, not on tablets of stone but on tablets of human hearts. (2 Cor. 2-3:3, NIV) I am an example (to believers) in word, in conduct, in love, in spirit, in faith, in purity. (1 Tim. 4:12)

F

I am faithfilled

What good is it…if I say I have faith but don't show it by my actions? Can that kind of faith save anyone? Suppose I see a brother or sister who has no food or clothing, and I say, "Good-bye and have a good day; stay warm and eat well"—but then I don't give that person any food or clothing. What good does that do? So… faith by itself isn't enough. Unless it produces good deeds, it is dead and useless. (James 2:14-17, NLT) Jesus said…if I say to this mountain, "Be removed and be cast into the sea," and do not doubt in my heart, but believe that those things I say will be done, I will have whatever I say… whatever things I ask when I pray, if I believe that I receive them, and I will have them. (Mark 11:23-24) If I have faith as a mustard seed, I will say to this mountain, "Move from here to there," and it will move; and nothing will be impossible for me. (Matt. 17:20) I live by faith, not by sight. (2 Cor. 5:7)

I am faithful; I am trustworthy; I am loyal; I am dependable

Whatever I do, I do it heartily, as to the Lord and not to men, knowing that from the Lord I will receive the reward of the inheritance; for I serve the Lord Christ. (Col. 3:23-24) If I am faithful in little things, I will be faithful in large ones. But if I am dishonest in little things, I won't be honest with greater responsibilities. And if I am untrustworthy about worldly wealth, who will trust me with the true riches of heaven? And if I am not faithful with other people's things, why should I be trusted with things of my own? (Luke 16:10-12, NLT) I will be faithful until death, and I will be given the crown of life. (Rev. 18:19)

15

I am favored
> *See also* - **I am blessed**

For it is by free grace (God's unmerited favor) that I am saved (delivered from judgment *and* made a partaker of Christ's salvation) through [my] faith. And this [salvation] is not of myself [of my own doing, it came not through my own striving], but it is the gift of God. (Eph. 2:7-8, Amp.)   I find favor, good understanding, and high esteem in the sight (judgment) of God and man. (Prov. 3:4, Amp.) For You, O LORD, will bless the righteous; with favor You will surround me as with a shield. (Psalm 5:12)

I am fearless
> *See also* - **I am courageous, I am strong**

God has not given me a spirit of fear, but of power and of love and of a sound mind. (2 Tim. 1:7)   I do not fear, for You are with me; I do not anxiously look about me, for You are my God. You will strengthen me, surely You will help me and uphold me with your righteous right hand. (Is. 41:10, NAS)   He who is in me is greater than he who is in the world. (1 John 4:4)

I am fervent (passionate)

Confess your trespasses to one another, and pray for one another, that you may be healed. The effective, fervent prayer of a righteous man avails much. (James 5:16) And above all things I have fervent love for others, for "love covers a multitude of sins." (1 Peter 4:8)

I am forgiven

I confess my sins, He is faithful and just to forgive me my sins and to cleanse me from all unrighteousness. (1 John 1:9) He has removed my sins as far from me as the east is from the west. (Psalm 103:12, NLT) When I was dead in my sins and in the uncircumcision of my flesh, God made me alive with Christ. He forgave me all my sins, having canceled the charge of my legal indebtedness, which stood against me and condemned me; he has taken it away, nailing it to the cross. (Col. 2:13-14, NIV)

I am forgiving

I will…stop being bitter and angry and mad at others. I won't…yell or curse or even be rude. Instead, I will be kind and merciful, forgiving others, just as God forgave me because of Christ. (Eph. 4:31-32, CEV) Love isn't selfish or quick tempered. It doesn't keep a record of wrongs that others do. (1 Cor. 13:5b, CEV)

I am free

Jesus said…If I abide in His Word, I am His disciple indeed. And I shall know the truth, and the truth shall make me free. (John 8:32) Now the Lord is the Spirit; and where the Spirit of the Lord is, there is liberty. (2 Corinthians 3:17) For the law of the Spirit of life in Christ Jesus has made me free from the law of sin and death. (Romans 8:2)

I am friendly

A friend is always loyal, and a brother is born to help in time of need. (Proverbs 17:17, NLT)   I have friends and I myself am friendly. (Prov. 18:24)

I am fruitful

But the Holy Spirit produces this kind of fruit in my life: love, joy, peace, patience, kindness, goodness, faithfulness, gentleness, and self-control. There is no law against these things! (Galatians 5:22-23, NLT) You (Jesus) are the Vine, I am the branch. I abide in You and You abide in me and I bear much fruit; for without You I can do nothing. (John 15:5) I do not cease to pray…and ask that I may be filled with the knowledge of His will in all wisdom and spiritual understanding; that I may walk worthy of the Lord, fully pleasing Him, being fruitful in every good work and increasing in the knowledge of God. (Col. 1:9-10)

I am fulfilled; I am complete
> *See also* - I am content; I am satisfied

The thief comes only in order to steal and kill and destroy. Jesus came that I may have and enjoy life, and have it in abundance (to the full, till it overflows). (John 10:10, Amplified) Jesus said to them, "I am the bread of life. He who comes to Me shall never hunger, and he who believes in Me shall never thirst. (John 6:35) May I experience the love of Christ, though it is so great I will never fully understand it. Then I will be filled with the fullness of life and power that comes from God. (Ephesians 3:19, NLT) For in Him dwells all the fullness of the Godhead bodily; and I am complete in Him, who is the head of all principality and power. (Colossians 2:9-10)

G

I am generous; I am sharing
> *See also* – **I am a giver**

The generous soul will be made rich and he who waters will also be watered himself. (Prov. 11:25)   John answered, "If you have two shirts, share with the person who does not have one. If you have food, share that also." (Luke 3:11, NCV)   I will do good, that I be rich in good works, ready to give, willing to share. (1 Timothy 6:18)

I am gifted

Having then gifts differing according to the grace that is given to me, I use them.   (Rom. 12:6a)   For God's gifts and His call are irrevocable. [He never withdraws them when once they are given, and He does not change His mind about those to whom He gives His grace or to whom He sends His call.]   (Romans 11:29, Amplified)

I am a giver; I am a receiver

I give as I purpose in my heart, not grudgingly or of necessity; for God loves a cheerful giver. (2 Cor. 9:7)   I give and it is given to me: good measure, pressed down, shaken together and running over will be put into my bosom.   For with the same measure I use, it will be measured back to me. (Luke 6:38)   Freely I have received, freely I give. (Matthew 10:8)   I remember the words of the Lord Jesus, that He said, "It is more blessed to give than to receive." (Acts 20:35)

I am God-fearing

For God has said, "I will never, never fail you nor forsake you."
That is why I can say without any doubt or fear, "The Lord is my
Helper, and I am not afraid of anything that mere man can do to me."
(Heb. 13:5b-6, TLB) The Lord said: "I, even I, am He who
comforts you. Who are you that you should be afraid of a man who
will die, and of the son of a man who will be made like grass?
(Isaiah 51:12) Fear of man is a dangerous trap, but to trust in God
means safety. (Proverbs 29:25, TLB)   The angel of the LORD
encamps all around those who fear Him, and delivers them. (Psalm
34:7)

I am a God pleaser

Do you think I am trying to make people accept me? No, God is the
only one I am trying to please. Am I trying to please people? If I
still wanted to please people, I would not be a servant of Christ. (Gal.
1:10, NCV) When a man's ways please the Lord, He makes even his
enemies to be at peace with him. (Proverbs 16:7) It's impossible to
please God apart from faith. And why? Because anyone who wants
to approach God must believe both that he exists *and* that he cares
enough to respond to those who seek him. (Hebrews 11:6, Msg)

I am gracious

My speech is always with grace, seasoned with salt, that I may know
how to answer each one. (Col. 4:6) I grow in grace (undeserved
favor, spiritual strength) and recognition and knowledge and
understanding of the Lord. (2 Peter 3:18, Amp.)   I am strong
(strengthened inwardly) in the grace (spiritual blessing) that is (to be
found) in Christ Jesus. (2 Tim. 2:1, Amplified)

H

I am happy; I am full of joy
> *See also* – I am fulfilled; I am complete

I have not seen Him, but still I love Him. I cannot see Him now, but I believe in Him. So I am filled with a joy that cannot be explained, a joy full of glory. (1 Peter 1:8, NCV) You will show me the path of life; In Your presence is fullness of joy; At Your right hand are pleasures forevermore. (Psalm 16:11) The joy of the Lord is my strength. (Neh. 8:10b) I have and enjoy life—in abundance (to the full, till it overflows). (John 10:10, Amplified)

I am healed
> *See also* – I am whole

Romans 8 : 11-17.

The Spirit of Him who raised Jesus from the dead dwells in me... and He gives life to my mortal body through His Spirit who dwells in me. (Romans 8:11) He bore my griefs and carried my sorrows...He was wounded for my transgressions. He was bruised for my iniquities; the chastisement for my peace was upon Him, and by His stripes I am healed. (Is. 53:4-5) And behold, a leper came and worshiped Him, saying, "Lord, if You are willing, You can make me clean." Then Jesus put out His hand and touched him, saying, "I am willing; be cleansed." Immediately his leprosy was cleansed. (Matthew 8:2-3)

I am healthy

A happy heart is good medicine *and* a cheerful mind works healing, but a broken spirit dries up the bones. (Proverbs 17:22, NCV) I am not wise in my own eyes; I fear the Lord and depart from evil. It is health to my flesh, and strength to my bones. (Prov. 3:7-8) Christ has redeemed me from the curse of the law (Gal. 3:13) ; therefore, I am in good health and every organ and every tissue of my body functions in the perfection to which God created it to function in the name of Jesus Christ.

I am heard

The righteous cry out, and the Lord hears, and delivers them out of all their troubles. (Psalm 34:17) Evening and morning and at noon I will pray, and cry aloud, and He shall hear my voice. (Psalm 55:17) For in You, O Lord, I hope; You will hear, O Lord my God. (Psalm 38:15) I sought the Lord, and He heard me, and delivered me from all my fears. (Psalm 34:4) I waited patiently for the Lord; And He inclined to me and heard my cry. (Psalm 40:1) I have heard your prayer, I have seen your tears; surely I will heal you. (2 Kings 20:5) This is the confidence I have in approaching God: that if I ask anything according to his will, he hears me. And if I know that he hears me—whatever I ask—I know that I have what I asked of him. (1 John 5:14-15, NIV)

I am hid
> *See also –* **I am safe**

For I died, and my life is hidden with Christ in God. (Col. 3:3) For in the time of trouble He shall hide me in His pavilion; in the secret place of His tabernacle He shall hide me; He shall set me high upon a rock. (Ps. 27:5) You are my hiding place; you will protect me from trouble and surround me with songs of deliverance. (Ps. 32:7)

I am holy

I present my body a living sacrifice, holy, acceptable to God, which is my reasonable service. (Rom. 12:1) As He who called me is holy, I also will be holy in all my conduct because it is written, "Be holy, for I am holy." (1 Peter 1:15-16)

I am Holy Spirit filled

I believe in Jesus, as the Scripture has said, and out of my heart flow rivers of living water. (John 7:37-38) I won't be drunk with wine, because that will ruin my life. Instead, I will be filled with the Holy Spirit. (Ephesians 5:18, NLT)

I am Holy Spirit led; I am directed

I let the Holy Spirit guide my life. Then I won't be doing what my sinful nature craves. The sinful nature wants to do evil, which is just the opposite of what the Spirit wants. And the Spirit gives me desires that are the opposite of what the sinful nature desires. These two forces are constantly fighting each other, so I am not free to carry out my good intentions. But when I am directed by the Spirit, I am not under obligation to the law of Moses. (Galatians 5:16-18, NLT) I live in the Spirit, I also walk in the Spirit. (Gal. 5:25) I trust in the Lord with all my heart, and lean not on my own understanding; in all my ways I acknowledge Him and He directs my paths. (Prov. 3:5-6) Tell me what to do, O Lord, and make it plain (because I am surrounded by waiting enemies). (Ps. 27:11, TLB) You instruct me and guide me along the best pathway for my life; You advise me and watch my progress. (Ps. 32:8, TLB) I will bless the Lord who counsels me; He gives me wisdom in the night. He tells me what to do. (Ps. 16:7, TLB) The LORD directs the steps of the godly. He delights in every detail of my life. (Psalm 37:23, NLT)

23

I am hopeful

Why are you cast down, O my soul? Any why are you disquieted within me? Hope in God; for I shall yet praise Him, the help of my countenance and my God. (Psalm 43:5) I wait for the Lord, my soul waits, and in His Word I do hope. (Ps. 130:5) The God of hope fills me with all joy and peace in believing, that I may abound in hope by the power of the Holy Spirit. (Rom. 15:13) The thoughts God thinks toward me are thoughts of peace and not of evil, to give me a future and a hope. (Jeremiah 29:11) This I recall to my mind, therefore I have hope. Through the LORD's mercies we are not consumed, because His compassions fail not. They are new every morning; great is Your faithfulness. "The LORD *is* my portion," says my soul, "Therefore I hope in Him!" The LORD is good to those who wait for Him, to the soul who seeks Him. It is good that one should hope and wait quietly for the salvation of the LORD. (Lamentations 3:21-26)

I am humble; I am lifted up

God resists the proud, but gives grace to the humble. Therefore I humble myself under the mighty hand of God, that He may exalt me in due time. (1 Peter 5:5-6) And He sat down, called the twelve, and said to them, "If anyone desires to be first, he shall be last of all and servant of all." (Mark 9:35) He must increase, but I must decrease. (He must grow more prominent; I must grow less so). (John 3:30, Amplified)

J-L

I am justified

Therefore having been justified by faith I have peace with God through my Lord Jesus Christ. (Romans 5:1) God demonstrates His own love toward me, in that while I was a sinner, Christ died for me. Much more then, having now been justified by His blood, I shall be saved from wrath through Him. (Rom. 5:8-9)

I am kind
> *See also* – I am loving, I am generous, I am compassionate, I am merciful

I am kindly affectionate to others with brotherly love, in honor giving preference to others. (Rom. 12:10) My own soul is nourished when I am kind. (Prov. 11:17a, TLB)

I am knowledgeable; I am understanding
> *See also* – I am wise

Lord, give to me the spirit of wisdom and revelation in the knowledge of You, the eyes of my understanding being enlightened; that I may know what is the hope of Your calling, what are the riches of the glory of Your inheritance in the saints. (Eph. 1:17-19) The entrance of Your Word gives light; it gives understanding to the simple. (Ps. 119:130) Let my cry come before You, O Lord; give me understanding according to Your Word. (Ps. 119:169)

I am the light of the world; I am the salt of the earth
> *See also* – I am an example

For once I was full of darkness, but now I have light from the Lord. So I live as a child of light! For this light within me produces only what is good and right and true. (Ephesians 5:8-9) I am the salt of the earth...I am the light of the world...I let my light shine before men, that they may see my good works and glorify my Father in heaven. (Matt. 5:13-16)

I am a good listener; I am a hearer; I am attentive; I am focused

I am quick to listen, slow to speak, and slow to get angry. (James 1:19, NLT) I look to Jesus, the one who began my faith and who makes it perfect. (Heb. 12:2-3, NCV) I give attention to Your Words; I incline my ear to your sayings. I do not let them depart from my eyes; I keep them in the midst of my heart. For they are life to me and health to all my flesh. (Prov. 4:20-22) So then faith comes by hearing, and hearing by the word of God. (Romans 10:17)

I am loved

And I am convinced that nothing can ever separate me from God's love. Neither death nor life, neither angels nor demons, neither my fears for today nor my worries about tomorrow—not even the powers of hell can separate me from God's love. No power in the sky above or in the earth below—indeed, nothing in all creation will ever be able to separate me from the love of God that is revealed in Christ Jesus my Lord. (Rom. 8:38-39) I keep His commandments and abide in His love. (John 15:10) I love Him because He first loved me. (1 John 4:19) For God so loved the world that He gave His only begotten Son, that whoever believes in Him should not perish but have everlasting life. (John 3:16)

I am loving
> *See also* – **I am rooted and grounded in love**

I love others, for love is of God and I am born of God and know God. (1 John 4:7-8) Love never fails. (1 Cor. 13:8a) All that I do is done in love. (1 Cor. 16:14, NAS) All who confess that Jesus is the Son of God have God living in them, and they live in God. I know how much God loves me, and I have put my trust in his love. God is love, and I who live in love live in God, and God lives in me. (1 John 4:15-16) Jesus replied, "The most important commandment is this: 'Listen, O Israel! The LORD our God is the one and only LORD. And you must love the LORD your God with all your heart, all your soul, all your mind, and all your strength. The second is equally important: 'Love your neighbor as yourself.' No other commandment is greater than these." (Mark 12:29-31, NLT)

M-O

I am mature

It's like this: When I was a child, I spoke and thought and reasoned as a child does. But when I grew up, I put away childish things. (1 Corinthians 13:11, NIV) I am confident of this very thing, that He who began a good work in me will perfect it until the day of Christ Jesus. (Philippians 1:6, NAS) I am growing in complete maturity of godliness in mind and character...as my heavenly Father is perfect. (Matt. 5:48, Amplified)

I am meek
> *See also* – **I am humble**

I am meek (mild, patient, long-suffering). I am blessed and shall inherit the earth. (Matt. 5:5, Amp.)

I am merciful > See also – I am compassionate

Blessed (happy, to be envied, and spiritually prosperous—with life-joy and satisfaction in God's favor and salvation, regardless of their outward conditions) are the merciful, for they shall obtain mercy! (Matthew 5:7, Amplified) For judgment is without mercy to the one who has shown no mercy. Mercy triumphs over judgment. (James 2:13) The merciful man does good for his own soul, but he who is cruel troubles his own flesh. (Proverbs 11:17) I am merciful (sympathetic, tender, responsive, and compassionate) even as my Father is (all these). (Luke 6:36, Amplified)

I am not judgmental

I judge not and I shall not be judged. I condemn not and I shall not be condemned. I forgive and I will be forgiven. (Luke 6:37) I will not speak evil against others. If I criticize and judge others, then I am criticizing and judging God's law. But my job is to obey the law, not to judge whether it applies to me. God alone, who gave the law, is the Judge. He alone has the power to save or to destroy. So what right do I have to judge my neighbor? (James 4:11-12, NLT)

I am obedient

But Samuel replied, "What is more pleasing to the LORD: your burnt offerings and sacrifices or your obedience to his voice? Listen! Obedience is better than sacrifice, and submission is better than offering the fat of rams. (1 Samuel 15:22, NLT) If I am willing and obedient, I shall eat the good of the land. (Isaiah 1:19) I realize that I become the slave of whatever I choose to obey. I can be a slave to sin, which leads to death, or I can choose to obey God, which leads to righteous living. (Romans 6:16, NLT) Because I love Him, I keep His commandments. (John 14:15)

I am occupying until He returns; I am productive

So I am careful how I live. I won't live like a fool, but like those who are wise. I make the most of every opportunity in these evil days. (Eph. 5:15-16, NLT) Teach me to number my days that I may gain a heart of wisdom. (Ps. 90:12) And whatever I do, I do it heartily, as to the Lord and not to men. (Colossians 3:23)

I am organized

For God is not the author of confusion, but of peace. (1 Corinthians 14:33a) God wants everything to be done peacefully and in order. (1 Corinthians 14:33, CEV)

I am an overcomer

He who is in me is greater than he who is in the world. (1 John 4:4b) I am of good cheer (I take courage; am confident, certain, undaunted)! For Jesus has overcome the world. (He has deprived it of its power to harm me and conquered it for me). (John 16:33, Amplified)

P

I am patient

I will wait on the Lord and renew my strength; I will mount up with wings like eagles, I will run and not be weary, I will walk and not faint. (Isaiah 40:31) I rest in the Lord and wait patiently for Him. (Ps. 37:7a) I let patience have its perfect work, that I may be perfect and complete, lacking nothing. (James 1:4) I waited patiently for the Lord to help me, and he turned to me and heard my cry. (Psalm 40:1, NLT)

I am a peacemaker

Peacemakers who sow in peace reap a harvest of righteousness. (James 3:18, NIV) For the Scriptures say, if I want to enjoy life and see many happy days, I must keep my tongue from speaking evil and my lips from telling lies. I turn away from evil and do good. I search for peace, and work to maintain it. (1 Peter 3:10-11, NLT) I pursue peace with all people, and holiness, without which no one will see the Lord. (Heb. 12:14)

I am perceptive; I am discerning

But Jesus perceived their wickedness... (Matthew 22:18) Lord, teach me good judgment, wise and right discernment and knowledge, for I believe Your commandments. (Psalms 119:66) I shall discern between the righteous and the wicked, between one who serves God and one who does not serve Him. (Malachi 3:18) The wise in heart are called discerning, and pleasant words promote instruction. (Proverbs 16:21, NIV) ...By reason of use I have my senses exercised to discern both good and evil. (Heb. 5:14)

33

I am persevering; I am able to endure

May I not grow weary while doing good, for in due season I shall reap if I do not lose heart. (Galatians 6:9) I remember that in a race everyone runs, but only one person gets the prize. I also must run in such a way that I will win. (1 Cor. 9:24, NLT) The temptations in my life are no different from what others experience. And God is faithful. He will not allow the temptation to be more than I can stand. When I am tempted, he will show me a way out so that I can endure. (1 Corinthians 10:13, NLT)

I am persistent; I am not giving up

I ask and it will be given to me; I seek and I will find; I knock and it will be opened to me. (Luke 11:8-9) Therefore, since I am surrounded by such a huge crowd of witnesses to the life of faith, I will strip off every weight that slows me down, especially the sin that so easily trips me up. And I will run with endurance the race God has set before me. I do this by keeping my eyes on Jesus, the champion who initiates and perfects my faith. Because of the joy awaiting him, he endured the cross, disregarding its shame. Now he is seated in the place of honor beside God's throne. I think of all the hostility he endured from sinful people; then I won't become weary and give up. (Hebrews 12:1-3, NLT)

I am positive; I am optimistic
> *See also* – **I am hopeful**

I'll do best by filling my mind and meditating on things that are true, noble, reputable, authentic, compelling, gracious –the best, not the worst, the beautiful, not the ugly; things to praise, not things to curse. (Phil 4:8, Msg) I set my mind on things above, not on things on the earth. (Colossians 3:2)

I am a prayer warrior
> *See also* – **I am armed**

And the Holy Spirit helps me in my weakness. For example, I don't know what God wants me to pray for. But the Holy Spirit prays for me with groanings that cannot be expressed in words. And the Father who knows all hearts knows what the Spirit is saying, for the Spirit pleads for us believers in harmony with God's own will. (Romans 8:26-27, NLT) I rejoice always, pray without ceasing, in everything I give thanks; for this is the will of God in Christ Jesus for me. (1 Thessalonians 5:16-18) I am human, but I do not wage war with human plans and methods. I use God's mighty weapons to knock down the devil's strongholds. With these weapons I break down every proud argument that keeps me from knowing God. (2 Cor. 10:3-5a, NLT) Confess your sins to each other and pray for each other so that you may be healed. The earnest prayer of a righteous person has great power and produces wonderful results. (James 5:16, NLT)

I am prosperous
> *See also* – **I am successful**

I am like a tree planted by the rivers of water, that brings forth its fruit in its season, whose leaf also shall not wither; and whatever I do shall prosper. (Psalm 1:3) I seek the Lord…and as long as I seek the Lord, God makes me to prosper. (2 Chron. 26:5)

I am prudent
> *See also* – **I am wise**

I have a heart of the prudent which acquires knowledge, and the ear of the wise which seeks knowledge. (Prov. 18:15) The simple believe anything, but the prudent give thought to their steps. (Proverbs 14:15, NIV)

R

I am reconciled to God

I once was alienated and an enemy in my mind by wicked works, yet now He has reconciled me in the body of His flesh through death, to present me holy, and blameless, and above reproach in His sight. (Col. 1:21-22) For if, while I was God's enemy, I was reconciled to him through the death of his Son, how much more, having been reconciled, shall I be saved through his life! Not only is this so, but I also boast in God through our Lord Jesus Christ, through whom I have now received reconciliation. (Romans 5:10-11, NIV) So now I can rejoice in my wonderful new relationship with God because my Lord Jesus Christ has made me a friend of God. (Romans 5:11, NLT)

I am redeemed

Christ has redeemed me from the curse of the law, having become a curse for me…The blessings of Abraham are come upon me in Christ Jesus. I receive the promise of the Spirit through faith. (Galatians 3:13-14) The Lord redeems the soul of His servants, and none of those who trust in Him shall be condemned. (Psalm 34:22) In Him I have redemption through His blood, the forgiveness of sins, according to the riches of His grace. (Ephesians 1:7)

I am refreshed; I am revived

He makes me lie down in (fresh, tender) green pastures; He leads me beside the still and restful waters. He refreshes and restores my life (my self). (Ps. 23:2-3a, Amp.) I am completely discouraged—I lie in the dust. Revive me by Your Word. (Ps. 119:25, TLB) Though I walk in the midst of trouble, You will revive me. (Psalm 138:7a)

Through the Lord's mercies I am not consumed, because His compassions fail not. They are new every morning; great is His faithfulness. (Lamentations 3:22-23)

I am reigning

I receive abundance of grace and the gift of righteousness and I will reign in life through the One, Jesus Christ. (Rom. 5:17) To Him who loved me and washed me from my sins in His own blood, and has made us kings and priests to His God and Father, to Him be glory and dominion forever and ever. Amen (Revelation 1:5b-6)

I am renewed; I am a new creation; I am transformed

Create in me a clean heart, O God, and renew a steadfast spirit within me. (Psalm 51:10) I am in Christ: I am a new creation; old things have passed away; behold, all things have become new. (2 Cor. 5:17) I throw off my old sinful nature and my former way of life, which is corrupted by lust and deception. Instead, I let the Spirit renew my thoughts and attitudes. I put on my new nature, created to be like God—truly righteous and holy. (Ephesians 4:22-24, NLT) I present my body a living sacrifice, holy, acceptable to God, which is my reasonable service. And I will not be conformed to this world, but I will be transformed by the renewing of my mind, that I may prove what is that good and acceptable and perfect will of God. (Romans 12:1-2) I am continually being renewed as I learn more and more about Christ, who created this new nature within me. (Colossians 3:9-10) I will not lose heart. Even though the outward man is perishing, yet the inward man is being renewed day by day. (2 Corinthians 4:16)

I am repentant

I *(Jesus)* have not come to call the righteous, but sinners to repentance. (Luke 5:32, NIV) If my people, which are called by my name, shall humble themselves, and pray, and seek my face, and turn from their wicked ways; then will I hear from heaven, and will forgive their sin, and will heal their land. (2 Chronicles 7:14) Search me, God, and know my heart; test me and know my anxious thoughts. (Psalm 139:23, NIV) Have mercy on me, O God, according to your unfailing love; according to your great compassion blot out my transgressions. (Psalm 51:1, NIV- *A psalm of David. When the prophet Nathan came to him after David had committed adultery with Bathsheba.*) I tell you that in the same way there will be more rejoicing in heaven over one sinner who repents than over ninety-nine righteous persons who do not need to repent. (Luke 15:7, NIV)

I am resilient

My steps are ordered by the Lord, and He delights in my way. Though I fall, I shall not be utterly cast down; for the Lord upholds me with His hand. (Psalm 37:23-24) For a righteous man may fall seven times and rise again, but the wicked shall fall by calamity. (Proverbs 24:16) The Lord upholds all those (of His own) who are falling and raises up all those who are bowed down. (Psalm 145:14, Amplified)

I am resting in God; I am relaxed; I am calm
> *See also* – I am trusting God

I come to You, weary and carrying heavy burdens and You give me rest. I take Your yoke upon me and learn from You…and I find rest for my soul. (Matt. 11:28-30) He makes me lie down in (fresh, tender) green pastures; He leads me beside the still and restful waters. (Psalm 23:2, Amplified) When I lie down, I will not be afraid; yes, I will lie down and my sleep will be sweet. (Prov. 3:24)

Therefore my heart is glad, and my glory rejoices; my flesh also will rest in hope. (Psalm 16:9) Accordingly then, I will not sleep, as the rest do, but I will keep wide awake (alert, watchful, cautious, and on my guard) and I will be sober (calm, collected, and circumspect). (1 Thessalonians 5:6, Amplified)

I am restored

You have allowed me to suffer much hardship, but you will restore me to life again and lift me up from the depths of the earth. You will restore me to even greater honor and comfort me once again. (Psalm 71:20-21, NLT) So I will restore to you the years that the swarming locust has eaten, The crawling locust, The consuming locust, And the chewing locust, My great army which I sent among you. (Joel 2:25)

I am reverent; I am respectful

I show respect for all people; I love the brothers and sisters of God's family, respect God, and honor the king. (1 Peter 2:17, NCV) Therefore, since I am receiving a kingdom that cannot be shaken, I will be thankful, and so worship God acceptably with reverence and awe. (Hebrews 12:28, NIV) Reverence for God gives a man deep strength; his children have a place of refuge and security. Reverence for the Lord is a fountain of life; its waters keep a man from death. (Proverbs 14:26-27, TLB)

I am righteous; I am sanctified

For He made Him who knew no sin to be sin for me, that I might become the righteousness of God in Him. (2 Cor. 5:21) God has united me with Christ Jesus. For my benefit God made him to be wisdom itself. Christ made me right with God; he made me pure and holy, and he freed me from sin. (1 Corinthians 1:30, NLT)

I am rooted and grounded in love
> *See also* – **I am loving**

Lord, strengthen me with might through Your Spirit in the inner man...that being rooted and grounded in love...I may know the love of Christ which passes knowledge and that I may be filled with all the fullness of God. (Eph. 3:16-19)   And now, just as I accepted Christ Jesus as my Lord, I must continue to follow him. I let my roots grow down into him, and let my life be built on him. Then my faith will grow strong in the truth I was taught, and I will overflow with thankfulness. (Colossians 2:6-7, NLT)   For all the law is fulfilled in one word, even in this: "You shall love your neighbor as yourself." (Galatians 5:14)   Where God's love is there is no fear, because God's perfect love drives out fear. It is punishment that makes me fear, so love is not made perfect in me when I fear. (1 John 4:18, NCV)

S

I am safe; I am protected
*> See also – **I am hid, I am secure***

Because I have made the Lord, who is my refuge, even the Most High, my dwelling place, no evil shall befall me, nor shall any plague come near my dwelling; For He shall give His angels charge over me, to keep me in all my ways. (Psalm 91:9-11) I listen to Him and dwell safely and am secure, without fear of evil. (Proverbs 1:33) May integrity and uprightness protect me, because my hope is in you. (Psalm 25:21, NIV) He who dwells in the secret place of the Most High shall abide under the shadow of the Almighty. I will say of the Lord, "He is my refuge and my fortress; my God, in Him I will trust." (Psalm 91:1-2) But the Lord is faithful, who will establish me and guard me from the evil one. (1 Thessalonians 3:3)

I am saved
*> See also –***I am a believer***

If I confess with my mouth that Jesus is Lord and believe in my heart that God raised him from the dead, I will be saved. For it is by believing in my heart that I am made right with God, and it is by confessing with my mouth that I am saved. (Romans 10:9-10, NLT) By grace I have been saved through faith, and that not of myself; it is the gift of God, not of works, lest I should boast. (Eph. 2:8-9) So they said, "Believe on the Lord Jesus Christ, and you will be saved, you and your household." (Acts 16:31)

I am sealed

Having believed, I was sealed with the Holy Spirit of promise. (Ephesians 1:13b) Now He who anointed me is God, who also has sealed me and given me the Spirit in my heart as a guarantee. (2 Cor.

1:21-22) And I will not grieve the Holy Spirit of God, by whom I was sealed for the day of redemption. (Ephesians 4:30)

I am secure
> *See also* – **I am safe**

For He Himself has said, "I will never leave you nor forsake you." So I may boldly say: "The Lord is my helper; I will not fear. What can man do to me?" (Heb. 13:5b-6) I listen to You and dwell safely and am secure without fear of evil. (Prov. 1:33) This I know, that God is for me. (Ps. 56:9, NAS)

I am a seeker

When You said, "Seek My face," My heart said to You, "Your face, LORD, I will seek." (Psalm 27:8) O God, You are my God; early will I seek You; my soul thirsts for You; my flesh longs for You in a dry and thirsty land where there is no water. (Psalm 63:1) I will seek You and find You when I search for You with all my heart. (Jeremiah 29:13) I ask, and it will be given to me; I seek, and I will find; I knock, and the door will be opened to me. (Matthew 7:6, NIV) I seek good and find favor, but evil comes to one who searches for it. (Proverbs 11:27)   I depart from evil and do good; I seek peace and pursue it. (Psalm 34:14) The young lions lack and suffer hunger; but those who seek the LORD shall not lack any good thing. (Psalm 34:10) I seek the kingdom of God, and all these things shall be added to me. (Luke 12:30-31)

I am self-controlled; I am self-disciplined

I put on the Lord Jesus Christ, and make no provision for the flesh, to fulfill its lusts (Rom. 13:14) In Christ I have crucified the flesh with its passions and desires. (Gal. 5:24) But the Holy Spirit produces this kind of fruit in our lives: love, joy, peace, patience, kindness, goodness, faithfulness, gentleness, and self-control. There is no law against these things! I who belong to Christ Jesus have nailed the passions and desires of my sinful nature to his cross and crucified them there. (Galatians 5:24, NLT) I walk in the Spirit and do not fulfill the lusts of the flesh. (Gal. 5:16-17)

I am a servant

I fear the Lord and serve Him in sincerity and in truth…I choose for myself this day whom I will serve…But as for me and my house, I will serve the Lord. (Joshua 24:14-15) I have been called to liberty; I will not use liberty as an opportunity for the flesh, but through love I will serve others. (Galatians 5:13) I serve the Lord and follow Him. Where He is I will be also. (John 12:26a) Whatever I do, I will work at it with all my heart, as working for the Lord, not for men, since I know that I will receive an inheritance from the Lord as a reward. It is the Lord I am serving. (Colossians 3:23-24, NIV)

I am skillful

Christ has given me special abilities—whatever He wants me to have out of His rich storehouse of gifts. (Eph. 4:7, TLB) I sing to Him a new song; I play skillfully with a shout of joy. (Psalm 33:3) …my tongue is the pen of a skillful writer. (Ps. 45:1, NIV)

I am slow to anger

I am swift to hear, slow to speak, slow to wrath. (James 1:19-20) When I am angry, I will not sin; I will not let the sun go down on my wrath, nor give place to the devil. (Ephesians 4:26-27) A hot-tempered man stirs up strife, but the slow to anger pacifies contention. (Proverbs 15:18, NAS) He who is slow to anger is better than the mighty, and he who rules his spirit than he who takes a city. (Proverbs 16:32)

I am a soul winner
> *See also* – I am a witness

I sing out His praises! I bless His name. Each day I tell someone He saves I publish His glorious acts throughout the earth. I tell everyone about the amazing things He does. (Psalm 96:2-3, TLB) I have become all things to all men, that I might by all means save some. (1 Corinthians 9:22b) The fruit of the righteous is a tree of life, and he who wins souls is wise. (Proverbs 11:30) And Jesus came and spoke to them, saying, "All authority has been given to Me in heaven and on earth. Go therefore and make disciples of all the nations, baptizing them in the name of the Father and of the Son and of the Holy Spirit, teaching them to observe all things that I have commanded you; and lo, I am with you always, even to the end of the age." Amen (Matthew 28:18-20)

I am sound minded; I am spiritually minded

I let the peace that comes from Christ control my thinking. (Col. 3:15b, NCV) In Thee, O Lord, do I put my trust: let me never be put to confusion. (Psalm 71:1, KJV) The peace of God that passes all understanding guards my heart and mind in Christ Jesus (Phil. 4:7) For God has not given me a spirit of fear, but of power and of love and of a sound mind. (2 Timothy 1:7) For to be carnally minded is death, but to be spiritually minded is life and peace. (Romans 8:6) I am human, but I don't wage war as humans do. I use God's mighty weapons, not worldly weapons, to knock down the strongholds of human reasoning and to destroy false arguments. I destroy every proud obstacle that keeps people from knowing God. I capture rebellious thoughts and teach them to obey Christ. (2 Corinthians 10:3-5, NLT)

I am special; I am unique; I am precious
> *See also* - **I am worthy**

I am His workmanship, created in Christ Jesus for good works, which God prepared beforehand that I should walk in them. (Eph. 2:10)   But I am part of a chosen generation, a royal priesthood, a holy nation, His own special people, that I may proclaim the praises of Him who called me out of darkness into His marvelous light. (1 Peter 2:9)   For You formed my inward parts; You covered me in my mother's womb. I will praise You, for I am fearfully and wonderfully made; marvelous are Your works, and that my soul knows very well. (Psalm 139:13-14)

I am stable; I am balanced

I am well balanced (temperate, sober of mind), and vigilant and cautious at all times; for that enemy of mine, the devil, roams around like a lion roaring (in fierce hunger) seeking someone to seize upon and devour. (1 Peter 5:8, Amp.) I know the LORD is always with me. I will not be shaken, for he is right beside me. (Psalm 16:8, NLT)   I will no longer be a little child, tossed and carried about by all kinds of teachings that change like the wind. I will no longer be influenced by people who use cunning and clever strategies to lead us astray. Instead, as I lovingly speak the truth, I will grow up completely in my relationship to Christ, who is the head. (Ephesians 4:14-15, GWT)

I am standing

I put on the whole armor of God that I may be able to stand against the wiles of the devil. (Ephesians 6:11) I watch and stand fast in the faith, being brave and strong. (1 Corinthians 16:13)

I am steadfast
> *See also* – I am persevering

You keep me in perfect peace (my mind is steadfast) because I trust in You. (Is. 26:3, NIV) This hope I have as an anchor of the soul, both sure and steadfast, and which enters the Presence behind the veil, where the forerunner has entered for us, even Jesus, having become High Priest forever according to the order of Melchizedek. (Hebrews 6:19-20)   I will be sober, be vigilant; because my adversary the devil walks about like a roaring lion, seeking whom he may devour. I resist him, steadfast in the faith, knowing that the same sufferings are experienced by my brotherhood in the world. (1 Peter 5:8-9) I will be steadfast, immovable, always abounding in the Lord, knowing that my labor is not in vain in the Lord. (1 Corinthians 15:58)

I am stirred up; I am motivated

I stir up the gift of God which is in me. (2 Timothy 1:6)   I build myself up on my most holy faith, praying in the Holy Ghost, I keep myself in the love of God, looking for the mercy of my Lord Jesus Christ unto eternal life. (Jude 20-21) [Not in my own strength] for it is God Who is all the while effectually at work in me [energizing and creating in me the power and desire], both to will and to work for His good pleasure and satisfaction and delight.   (Philippians 2:13, Amplified)

I am strong

The Lord is the strength of my life; of whom shall I be afraid? (Ps. 27:16) I do not sorrow, for the joy of the Lord is my strength. (Nehemiah 8:10) I am strong and of good courage; I am not afraid nor dismayed, for the Lord my God is with me wherever I go. (Josh.1:9)   I am strong in the Lord and in the power of His might. (Eph. 6:10)   I can do all things through Christ who strengthens me.

(Phil. 4:13) I wait on the Lord and He renews my strength; I shall mount up with wings like eagles, I shall run and not be weary, I shall walk and not faint. (Isaiah 40:30-31)

I am submissive

I submit to God. I resist the devil and he flees from me. I draw near to God and He draws near to me. (James 4:7-8a) Likewise you younger people, submit yourselves to your elders. Yes, all of you be submissive to one another, and be clothed with humility, for "God resists the proud, but gives grace to the humble." (1 Peter 5:5) Everyone must submit to governing authorities. For all authority comes from God, and those in positions of authority have been placed there by God. So anyone who rebels against authority is rebelling against what God has instituted, and they will be punished. For the authorities do not strike fear in people who are doing right, but in those who are doing wrong. Would you like to live without fear of the authorities? Do what is right, and they will honor you. The authorities are God's servants, sent for your good. But if you are doing wrong, of course you should be afraid, for they have the power to punish you. They are God's servants, sent for the very purpose of punishing those who do what is wrong. So you must submit to them, not only to avoid punishment, but also to keep a clear conscience. (Romans 13:1-5, NLT) Submit to one another out of reverence for Christ. (Ephesians 5:21, NIV)

I am successful
> *See also –* **I am prosperous**

I commit to the Lord whatever I do, and my plans will succeed. (Prov. 16:3, NIV) This Book of the Law shall not depart from my mouth, but I shall meditate in it day and night, that I may observe to do according to all that is written in it. For then my way will be prosperous, and then I will have good success. (Joshua 1:8)

T

I am teachable

I take firm hold of instruction, I do not let go; I keep her, for she is my life. (Prov. 4:13)   The Holy Spirit teaches me all things and brings to my remembrance all things that Jesus said to me.   (John 14:26) Rebuke a wise man, and he will love you.   Give instruction to a wise man, and he will be still wiser; teach a just man, and he will increase in learning.   (Proverbs 9:8b-9)   He who disdains instruction despises his own soul, but he who heeds rebuke gets understanding. (Proverbs 15:32)

I am tenacious

I hold fast the confession of my hope without wavering; for He who promised is faithful. (Hebrews 10:23)   I test all things and hold fast what is good. (1 Thessalonians 5:21)

I am thankful; I am appreciative; I am grateful

I rejoice always, pray without ceasing, and in everything give thanks; for this is the will of God in Christ Jesus for me. (1 Thess. 5:16-18) I don't worry about anything; instead, I pray about everything; I tell God my needs, and I thank Him for His answers. (Phil. 4:6, TLB)   I give thanks to the Lord, for He is good!   For His mercy endures forever. (Psalm 107:1)   Therefore by Him I will continually offer the sacrifice of praise to God, that is, the fruit of my lips, giving thanks to His name.   (Hebrews 13:15)   And I let the peace that comes from Christ rule in my heart. For as a member of one body I am called to live in peace. And always be thankful.   (Colossians 3:15, NLT)

I am a tither

I honor the Lord with my possessions, and with the first fruits of all my increase; so my barns will be filled with plenty and my vats will overflow with new wine. (Prov. 3:9-10) I sow bountifully and will also reap bountifully. So I give as I purpose in my heart, not grudgingly or of necessity; for God loves a cheerful giver. (2 Cor. 9:6-7) "Bring all the tithes into the storehouse, that there may be food in My house, and try Me now in this," says the LORD of hosts, "If I will not open for you the windows of heaven and pour out for you such blessing that there will not be room enough to receive it. And I will rebuke the devourer for your sakes, so that he will not destroy the fruit of your ground, nor shall the vine fail to bear fruit for you in the field," says the LORD of hosts; "And all nations will call you blessed, for you will be a delightful land," says the LORD of hosts. (Malachi 3:10-12)

I am triumphant
> *See also* – **I am victorious**

For You Lord have made me glad through Your work; I will triumph in the works of Your hands. (Psalm 92:4) But thanks be to God! He has made us his captives and continues to lead us along in Christ's triumphal procession. Now he uses us to spread the knowledge of Christ everywhere, like a sweet perfume. (2 Corinthians 2:14, NLT) The Lord is with me; he is my helper. I look in triumph on my enemies. (Psalm 118:7, NLT)

I am trusting God

You keep me in perfect peace; my mind is stayed on you; because I trust in You. (Isaiah 26:3) I trust in the Lord with all my heart and lean not on my own understanding; in all my ways I acknowledge Him, and He shall direct my paths. (Prov. 3:5-7) I trust in the Lord and am like Mt. Zion, which cannot be moved, but abides forever. (Ps. 125:1)

I am truthful; I am honest; I am genuine

I walk in truth. (3 John 4) Jesus said if I abide in His word, I am His disciple indeed. And I shall know the truth, and the truth shall make me free. (John 8:31-32) Lying lips are an abomination to the Lord, but those who deal truthfully are His delight. (Proverbs 12:22)

V

I am a vessel of honor

For God, who said, "Let there be light in the darkness," has made this light shine in our hearts so we could know the glory of God that is seen in the face of Jesus Christ. We now have this light shining in our hearts, but we ourselves are like fragile clay jars containing this great treasure. This makes it clear that our great power is from God, not from ourselves. (2 Corinthians 4:6-7, NLT)

I am victorious
> *See also* – **I am triumphant**

Yet amid all these things I am more than a conqueror and I gain a surpassing victory through Him Who loved me. (Rom. 8:37, Amplified)   I am not afraid or discouraged because of this vast army. For the battle is not mine, but God's. (2 Chron. 20:15b) But thanks be to God, who gives us the victory through our Lord Jesus Christ. (1 Corinthians 15:57)

I am vindicated

For You have judged in my favor; from Your throne You have judged with fairness. (Psalm 9:4, NLT)   You will establish me in the end (keep me steadfast, give me strength, and guarantee my vindication; You will be my warrant against all accusation or indictment so that I will be) guiltless and irreproachable in the day of my Lord Jesus Christ (the Messiah). (1 Corinthians 1:8, Amplified)

I am virtuous

I shun youthful lusts and flee from them, and aim at and pursue righteousness (all that is virtuous and good, right living, conformity to the will of God in thought, word, and deed); [and aim at and pursue] faith, love, [and] peace (harmony and concord with others) in fellowship with all [Christians], who call upon the Lord out of a pure heart. (2 Timothy 2:22, Amplified) I must be perfect (grow in complete maturity of godliness in mind and character, having reached the proper height of virtue and integrity), as my heavenly Father is perfect. (Matt. 5:48, Amplified) For this very reason, adding your diligence [to the divine promises], I employ every effort in exercising my faith to develop virtue (excellence, resolution, Christian energy), and in [exercising] virtue [develop] knowledge (intelligence). (2 Peter 1:5, Amplified)

I am visionary

Lord, You said you will pour out of Your Spirit on all flesh; our sons and daughters will prophesy, young men shall see visions, old men shall dream dreams. (Acts 2:17) Where there is no vision, the people perish; but he that keepeth the law, happy is he. (Proverbs 29:18, KJV)

W

I am waiting on God

I wait for the Lord, my soul waits, and in His Word I do hope. (Ps. 130:5) In the morning You hear my voice, O Lord; in the morning I prepare (a prayer, a sacrifice) for You, and watch and wait (for You to speak to my heart). (Ps. 5:3, Amplified) I wait on the Lord and he renews my strength; I shall mount up with wings as eagles, I shall run and not be weary, I shall walk and not faint. (Isaiah 40:31)

I am walking with God

As I have, therefore, received Christ Jesus the Lord, so I walk in Him, rooted and built up in Him and established in the faith, as I have been taught, abounding in it with thanksgiving. (Col. 2:6-7) My eyes will be on the faithful in the land that they may dwell with me; he whose walk is blameless will minister to me. (Psalm 101:6) He who walks righteously and speaks uprightly, who despises gain from fraud and from oppression, who shakes his hand free from the taking of bribes, who stops his ears from hearing of bloodshed and shuts his eyes to avoid looking upon evil. [Such a man] will dwell on the heights; his place of defense will be the fortresses of rocks; his bread will be given him; water for him will be sure. (Isaiah 33:15-16, Amplified)

I am wealthy

I seek first the kingdom of God and His righteousness and all these things shall be added to me. (Matt. 6:33) And I shall remember the Lord my God, for it is He who gives me power to get wealth, that He may establish His covenant which He swore to my fathers, as it is this day. (Deut. 8:18) And my God shall supply all my need according to His riches in glory by Christ Jesus. (Philippians 4:19) Wealth [not earned but] won in haste *or* unjustly *or* from the production of things for vain *or* detrimental use [such riches] will dwindle away, but he who gathers little by little will increase [his riches]. (Proverbs 13:11, Amplified)

I am whole
> *See also* – **I am healed**

May God sanctify me completely; and may my whole spirit, soul and body be preserved blameless at the coming of our Lord Jesus Christ. (1 Thess. 5:23) And he said to her, "Daughter, be of good comfort; thy faith hath made thee whole; go in peace. (Luke 8:48, KJV)

I am a winner

Those who run in a race all run, but only one receives the prize. I run in such a way that I may win. (1 Corinthians 9:24, NAS) I press on toward the goal to win the prize for which God has called me heavenward in Christ Jesus. (Phil. 3:14, NIV) I fight the good fight for the true faith. I hold tightly to the eternal life to which God has called me, which I have confessed so well before many witnesses. (1Timothy 6:12) Yes, everything else is worthless when compared with the infinite value of knowing Christ Jesus my Lord. For his sake I have discarded everything else, counting it all as garbage, so that I could gain Christ (Philippians 3:8, NLT)

I am wise

If I lack wisdom, I ask God who gives liberally and without reproach. (James 1:5) The entrance of Your words gives light; it gives understanding to the simple. (Psalm 119:130) I will not be wise in my own eyes; I fear the Lord and turn away from evil.

(Proverbs 3:7, NAS)   Fear of the LORD is the foundation of true wisdom. All who obey his commandments will grow in wisdom. Praise him forever! (Psalm 111:10)

I am a witness; I am an ambassador for Christ

I received power when the Holy Spirit came upon me; and I am a witness to Jesus. (Acts 1:8) So I am Christ's ambassador; God is making his appeal through me. I speak for Christ when I plead, "Come back to God!" (2 Corinthians 5:20, NLT)

I am a worshipper

I am a true worshipper and I worship the Father in spirit and in truth. (John 4:23-24) I will praise You with music, telling of Your faithfulness to all Your promises, O Holy One of Israel. I will shout and sing Your praises for redeeming me. (Psalm 71:22-23, TLB) I will bless the Lord at all times; His praise shall continually be in my mouth. (Psalm 34:1)   I exalt the Lord my God, and worship at His footstool—He is holy. (Psalm 99:5) Praise the Lord. Praise the Lord, O my soul. I will praise the Lord all my life; I will sing praise to my God as long as I live. (Psalm 146:1-2, NIV)

I am worthy; I am significant; I am important; I am valuable
> *See also* – I am loved, I am a child of God, I am special

But the very hairs of my head are all numbered. Therefore, I do not fear; I am of more value than many sparrows. (Matthew 10:30-31) If a man has a hundred sheep and one of them wanders away, what will he do? Won't he leave the ninety-nine others on the hills and go out to search for the one that is lost? And if he finds it, I tell you the truth, he will rejoice over it more than over the ninety-nine that didn't wander away! In the same way, it is not my heavenly Father's will that even one of these little ones should perish. (Matthew 18:12-15, NLT) His son said to him, "Father, I have sinned against both heaven and you, and I am no longer worthy of being called your son." But his father said to the servants, "Quick! Bring the finest robe in the house and put it on him. Get a ring for his finger and sandals for his feet. And kill the calf we have been fattening. We must celebrate with a feast, for this son of mine was dead and has now returned to life. He was lost, but now he is found." So the party began. (Luke 15:21-24, NLT)

31 DAY READING GUIDE
for Study & Meditation

In Christ, I Am can be used as part of a Bible Study to empower the believer. On a daily (or weekly) basis, read through the *In Christ, I Am's* listed below. Study, meditate and pray over all the confessions and Scriptures. You may also want to journal your personal experiences and insight. This practice will not only help you understand your identity in Christ, it will strengthen your faith and deepen your walk with the Lord.

Never stop reciting these teachings. You must think about them night and day so that you will faithfully do everything written in them. Only then will you prosper and succeed. (Joshua 1:8, GW)

☐ **Day 1**
I AM ABOVE ONLY AND NOT BENEATH/
  I AM THE HEAD NOT THE TAIL
I AM ABOVE PROBLEMS
I AM ACCEPTED IN THE BELOVED
I AM ACCOUTABLE; I AM RESPONSIBLE

☐ **Day 2**
I AM ANOINTED
I AM ARMED
I AM BEAUTIFUL
I AM A BELIEVER

☐ **Day 3**
I AM BLESSED
I AM BOLD
I AM BUILDING MY SPIRITUAL HOUSE
I AM CALLED

☐ **Day 4**
I AM CAREFREE/I AM ANXIOUS FOR NOTHING
I AM CAREFUL OF WHAT I SAY
I AM A CHILD OF GOD/I AM A JOINT HEIR
I AM CHOSEN

☐ Day 5
I AM CHRIST-LIKE
I AM CLEAN/I AM PURE IN HEART
I AM COMFORTED
I AM COMFORTING OTHERS

☐ Day 6
I AM COMPASSIONATE; CARING; EMPATHETIC
I AM CONFIDENT
I AM CONTENT/I AM SATISFIED
I AM COURAGEOUS

☐ Day 7
I AM CREATED/I AM MADE IN GOD'S IMAGE
I AM CREATIVE
I AM DEAD TO SIN/I AM RISEN
I AM DEBT-FREE
I AM DEVOTED; I AM DEDICATED

☐ Day 8
I AM DILIGENT
I AM A DISCIPLE OF CHRIST/ I AM LIVING FOR CHRIST
I AM A DOER OF THE WORD
I AM EMPOWERED

☐ Day 9
I AM ENCOURAGED/ I AM EDIFIED
I AM ENCOURAGING OTHERS
I AM EQUIPPED/PREPARED/CAPABLE/ABLE
I AM ETERNAL

☐ Day 10
I AM AN EXAMPLE
I AM FAITHFILLED
I AM FAITHFUL/TRUSTWORTHY/LOYAL/DEPENDABLE
I AM FAVORED

☐ Day 11
I AM FEARLESS
I AM FERVENT
I AM FORGIVEN
I AM FORGIVING
I AM FREE

☐ Day 12
I AM FRIENDLY
I AM FRUITFUL
I AM FULFILLED/I AM COMPLETE
I AM GENEROUS/I AM SHARING
I AM GIFTED

☐ Day 13
I AM A GIVER/I AM A RECEIVER
I AM GOD-FEARING
I AM A GOD PLEASER
I AM GRACIOUS

☐ Day 14
I AM HAPPY/ I AM FULL OF JOY
I AM HEALED
I AM HEALTHY
I AM HEARD
I AM HID

☐ Day 15
I AM HOLY
I AM HOLY SPIRIT FILLED
I AM HOLY SPIRIT LED/DIRECTED
I AM HOPEFUL
I AM HUMBLE/I AM LIFTED UP

☐ Day 16
I AM JUSTIFIED
I AM KIND
I AM KNOWLEDGEABLE/I AM UNDERSTANDING
I AM THE LIGHT OF THE WORLD/ SALT OF THE EARTH

☐ Day 17
I AM A LISTENER/ HEARER/ ATTENTIVE/ FOCUSED
I AM LOVED
I AM LOVING
I AM MATURE
I AM MEEK

☐ Day 18
I AM MERCIFUL
I AM NOT JUDGEMENTAL
I AM OBEDIENT
I AM OCCUPYING UNTIL HE RETURNS/I AM PRODUCTIVE
I AM ORGANIZED

☐ Day 19
I AM AN OVERCOMER
I AM PATIENT
I AM A PEACEMAKER
I AM PERCEPTIVE/I AM DISCERNING
I AM PERSERVERING/I AM ABLE TO ENDURE

☐ Day 20
I AM PERSISTENT/I AM NOT GIVING UP
I AM POSITIVE AND OPTIMISTIC
I AM A PRAYER WARRIOR
I AM PROSPEROUS

☐ Day 21
I AM PRUDENT
I AM RECONCILED TO GOD
I AM REDEEMED
I AM REFRESHED/I AM REVIVED
I AM REIGNING

☐ Day 22
I AM RENEWED/I AM A NEW CREATION/I AM TRANSFORMED
I AM REPENTANT
I AM RESILIENT
I AM RESTING IN GOD/RELAXED/CALM
I AM RESTORED

☐ Day 23
I AM REVERENT/ RESPECTFUL
I AM RIGHTEOUS/I AM SANCTIFIED
I AM ROOTED AND GROUNDED IN LOVE
I AM SAFE/ I AM PROTECTED
I AM SAVED

☐ Day 24
I AM SEALED
I AM SECURE
I AM A SEEKER
I AM SELF-CONTROLLED/I AM SELF-DISCIPLINED

☐ Day 25
I AM A SERVANT
I AM SKILLFUL
I AM SLOW TO ANGER
I AM A SOUL WINNER
I AM SOUND-MINDED/I AM SPIRITUALLY MINDED

☐ Day 26

I AM SPECIAL/UNIQUE/PRECIOUS
I AM STABLE/BALANCED
I AM STANDING
I AM STEADFAST
I AM STIRRED UP/I AM MOTIVATED

☐ Day 27

I AM STRONG
I AM SUBMISSIVE
I AM SUCCESSFUL
I AM TEACHABLE
I AM TENACIOUS

☐ Day 28

I AM THANKFUL/I AM APPRECIATIVE/I AM GRATEFUL
I AM A TITHER
I AM TRIUMPHANT
I AM TRUSTING GOD
I AM TRUTHFUL/ HONEST/ GENUINE

☐ Day 29

I AM A VESSEL OF HONOR
I AM VICTORIOUS
I AM VINDICATED
I AM VIRTUOUS
I AM VISIONARY

☐ Day 30

I AM WAITING ON GOD
I AM WALKING WITH GOD
I AM WEALTHY
I AM WHOLE
I AM A WINNER

☐ Day 31

I AM WISE
I AM A WITNESS/AMBASSADOR
I AM A WORSHIPPER
I AM WORTHY/ SIGNIFICANT/ IMPORTANT/ VALUABLE

Checklist of Every IN CHRIST, I AM…

- ☐ I AM ABOVE ONLY AND NOT BENEATH/
  I AM THE HEAD NOT THE TAIL

- ☐ I AM ABOVE PROBLEMS

- ☐ I AM ACCEPTED IN THE BELOVED

- ☐ I AM ACCOUTABLE; I AM RESPONSIBLE

- ☐ I AM ANOINTED

- ☐ I AM ARMED

- ☐ I AM BEAUTIFUL

- ☐ I AM A BELIEVER

- ☐ I AM BLESSED

- ☐ I AM BOLD

- ☐ I AM BUILDING MY SPIRITUAL HOUSE

- ☐ I AM CALLED

- ☐ I AM CAREFREE/I AM ANXIOUS FOR NOTHING

- ☐ I AM CAREFUL OF WHAT I SAY

- ☐ I AM A CHILD OF GOD/I AM A JOINT HEIR

- ☐ I AM CHOSEN

- ☐ I AM CHRIST-LIKE

- ☐ I AM CLEAN/I AM PURE IN HEART

- ☐ I AM COMFORTED

- ☐ I AM COMFORTING OTHERS

- ☐ I AM COMPASSIONATE; CARING; EMPATHETIC

- ☐ I AM CONFIDENT
- ☐ I AM CONTENT/I AM SATISFIED
- ☐ I AM COURAGEOUS
- ☐ I AM CREATED/I AM MADE IN GOD'S IMAGE
- ☐ I AM CREATIVE
- ☐ I AM DEAD TO SIN/I AM RISEN
- ☐ I AM DEBT-FREE
- ☐ I AM DEVOTED; I AM DEDICATED
- ☐ I AM DILIGENT
- ☐ I AM A DISCIPLE OF CHRIST/ I AM LIVING FOR CHRIST
- ☐ I AM A DOER OF THE WORD
- ☐ I AM EMPOWERED
- ☐ I AM ENCOURAGED/ I AM EDIFIED
- ☐ I AM ENCOURAGING OTHERS
- ☐ I AM EQUIPPED/PREPARED/CAPABLE/ABLE
- ☐ I AM ETERNAL
- ☐ I AM AN EXAMPLE
- ☐ I AM FAITHFILLED
- ☐ I AM FAITHFUL/TRUSTWORTHY/LOYAL/DEPENDABLE
- ☐ I AM FAVORED
- ☐ I AM FEARLESS
- ☐ I AM FERVENT
- ☐ I AM FORGIVEN

- [ ] I AM FORGIVING
- [ ] I AM FREE
- [ ] I AM FRIENDLY
- [ ] I AM FRUITFUL
- [ ] I AM FULFILLED/I AM COMPLETE
- [ ] I AM GENEROUS/I AM SHARING
- [ ] I AM GIFTED
- [ ] I AM A GIVER/I AM A RECEIVER
- [ ] I AM GOD-FEARING
- [ ] I AM A GOD PLEASER
- [ ] I AM GRACIOUS
- [ ] I AM HAPPY/ I AM FULL OF JOY
- [ ] I AM HEALED
- [ ] I AM HEALTHY
- [ ] I AM HEARD
- [ ] I AM HID
- [ ] I AM HOLY
- [ ] I AM HOLY SPIRIT FILLED
- [ ] I AM HOLY SPIRIT LED/DIRECTED
- [ ] I AM HOPEFUL
- [ ] I AM HUMBLE/I AM LIFTED UP
- [ ] I AM JUSTIFIED
- [ ] I AM KIND

- [ ] I AM KNOWLEDGEABLE/I AM UNDERSTANDING
- [ ] I AM THE LIGHT OF THE WORLD/ SALT OF THE EARTH
- [ ] I AM A LISTENER/ HEARER/ ATTENTIVE/ FOCUSED
- [ ] I AM LOVED
- [ ] I AM LOVING
- [ ] I AM MATURE
- [ ] I AM MEEK
- [ ] I AM MERCIFUL
- [ ] I AM NOT JUDGEMENTAL
- [ ] I AM OBEDIENT
- [ ] I AM OCCUPYING UNTIL HE RETURNS/I AM PRODUCTIVE
- [ ] I AM ORGANIZED
- [ ] I AM AN OVERCOMER
- [ ] I AM PATIENT
- [ ] I AM A PEACEMAKER
- [ ] I AM PERCEPTIVE/I AM DISCERNING
- [ ] I AM PERSERVERING/I AM ABLE TO ENDURE
- [ ] I AM PERSISTENT/I AM NOT GIVING UP
- [ ] I AM POSITIVE AND OPTIMISTIC
- [ ] I AM A PRAYER WARRIOR
- [ ] I AM PROSPEROUS
- [ ] I AM PRUDENT
- [ ] I AM RECONCILED TO GOD

- ☐ I AM REDEEMED

- ☐ I AM REFRESHED/I AM REVIVED

- ☐ I AM REIGNING

- ☐ I AM RENEWED/I AM A NEW CREATION/I AM TRANSFORMED

- ☐ I AM REPENTANT

- ☐ I AM RESILIENT

- ☐ I AM RESTING IN GOD/RELAXED/CALM

- ☐ I AM RESTORED

- ☐ I AM REVERENT/ RESPECTFUL

- ☐ I AM RIGHTEOUS/I AM SANCTIFIED

- ☐ I AM ROOTED AND GROUNDED IN LOVE

- ☐ I AM SAFE/ I AM PROTECTED

- ☐ I AM SAVED

- ☐ I AM SEALED

- ☐ I AM SECURE

- ☐ I AM A SEEKER

- ☐ I AM SELF-CONTROLLED/I AM SELF-DISCIPLINED

- ☐ I AM A SERVANT

- ☐ I AM SKILLFUL

- ☐ I AM SLOW TO ANGER

- ☐ I AM A SOUL WINNER

- ☐ I AM SOUND-MINDED/I AM SPIRITUALLY MINDED

- ☐ I AM SPECIAL/UNIQUE/PRECIOUS

- ☐ I AM STABLE/BALANCED
- ☐ I AM STANDING
- ☐ I AM STEADFAST
- ☐ I AM STIRRED UP/I AM MOTIVATED
- ☐ I AM STRONG
- ☐ I AM SUBMISSIVE
- ☐ I AM SUCCESSFUL
- ☐ I AM TEACHABLE
- ☐ I AM TENACIOUS
- ☐ I AM THANKFUL/I AM APPRECIATIVE/I AM GRATEFUL
- ☐ I AM A TITHER
- ☐ I AM TRIUMPHANT
- ☐ I AM TRUSTING GOD
- ☐ I AM TRUTHFUL/ HONEST/ GENUINE
- ☐ I AM A VESSEL OF HONOR
- ☐ I AM VICTORIOUS
- ☐ I AM VINDICATED
- ☐ I AM VIRTUOUS
- ☐ I AM VISIONARY
- ☐ I AM WAITING ON GOD
- ☐ I AM WALKING WITH GOD
- ☐ I AM WEALTHY
- ☐ I AM WHOLE

- ☐ I AM A WINNER

- ☐ I AM WISE

- ☐ I AM A WITNESS/AMBASSADOR FOR CHRIST

- ☐ I AM A WORSHIPPER

- ☐ I AM WORTHY/ SIGNIFICANT/ IMPORTANT/ VALUABLE

Are You in Christ
And Is Christ In You?

Jesus Christ has made the Father God known to us: *"I have made You known to them, and will continue to make You known in order that the love You have for Me may be in them and that I Myself may be in them"* (John 17:26, NIV). God wants us to receive His love. In doing so, we will be in Christ and He will be in us.

First, it must be understood that God's love is freely given to us in His Son and His love holds no conditions. There is nothing you can do to EARN God's love. It doesn't matter how many times or how hard you try to be a good person or live a worthy life. "For by **GRACE** you have been saved through **FAITH**, and that not of yourselves; it is the **GIFT OF GOD**, not of works, lest anyone should boast" (Ephesians 2:8-9). Salvation is a gift of God. It is not our   reward for doing good things on earth.

Secondly, we must recognize that we "all fall short of God's glorious ideal" (Romans 3:23, TLB). We ALL have sinned and there is punishment for sin. God doesn't want us to face the eternal judgment for sin; that is why He sent His Son. Jesus Christ paid the price for our sin and redeemed us with His precious blood (1 Peter 1:18-19). In order to be saved, we must acknowledge our sin and repent.

The Bible says you can choose to be in Christ. You can choose to go from eternal death (separation from God) to eternal life: "If you *confess* with your mouth the Lord Jesus and *believe* in your heart that God has raised Him from the dead, you will be saved. For with the heart one believes unto righteousness and with the mouth confession
is made unto salvation" (Romans 10:9-10).

If you want to be sure that you are in Christ
and that He is in you then pray this prayer to God:

Dear Heavenly Father.....

I come to you in the name of Jesus. I confess I am a sinner and come short of the glory of God (Romans 3:23). I repent and ask for Your forgiveness. I believe in my heart Jesus Christ is the Son of God. I believe He was raised from the dead for my justification. And I confess Him now as my Lord and Savior (Romans 10:9-10). The blood of Jesus Christ has cleansed me from all sin (1 John 1:7) and now I am a child of God and I am saved (John 1:12).
Thank You, Lord!!

What's next?

1- **Pray** every day (talk to God; He hears you).

2- **Read** the Bible every day.

3- Get rooted and grounded in a Bible-believing **church**.

About the Authors

Since 1989, Krystal and Violet have been sharing and ministering God's love, hope, healing and encouragement through their books, articles, websites, businesses, music ministry and outreaches.

Krystal Kuehn, MA, LPC, LLP, NCC is a psychotherapist, best-selling author, teacher, and musician.

Krystal specializes in helping people live their best life now, reach their full potential, overcome barriers, heal from their past, & develop a happiness lifestyle. Her inspirational and empowering approach has been helping people all over the world for over 20 years. Krystal's articles, poetry, and songs have been published locally and internationally. She is also the author of many books.
For a Complete List go to:
http://www.amazon.com/author/krystalkuehn

Krystal has a passion for encouraging others. She believes everyone has untapped potential for greatness and everyone can live a life of fulfillment and true happiness. Krystal is the co-founder of New Day Counseling in Michigan. Her web sites include:

Christian-Kindle-Books.com
NewDayCounseling.org
NewDayHealthyLiving.com
NewDayCounselingCenter.blogspot.com
Facebook.com/WordsofInspiration
ChristianWalk.net
Baby-Poems.com
NewSongProductions.com
BeHappy4Life.com
NewDayMusicOutreach.com

Connect with Krystal Kuehn

It is my sincerest desire and hope that *In Christ, I am - God's Promises on Who You are in Christ that Will Transform You from the Inside Out* has enriched your life and provided you with empowering promises from God's word to help change from the inside out and know who you are in Him! I would love to hear your testimonials and how you have been blessed. You can send your testimonials, feedback and comments to me at:

maxpotential312@gmail.com

If you would like to share your experience with others, I would truly appreciate if you would write a review on Amazon.com.

My author profile:
http://www.amazon.com/author/krystalkuehn

Join my *Words of Inspiration* page and Friend me on Facebook: http://www.facebook.com/WordsOfInspiration

Follow and connect with me on Twitter:
http://www.twitter.com/behappy4lifeNDC

Visit my *Be Your Best* blog (offers RSS):
http://www.newdaycounselingcenter.blogspot.com

Violet James, MSM is an entrepreneur, marketing and business manager, award-winning web designer, and artist. She is the cofounder of NewDayCounseling.org, NewDayHealthyLiving.com, Christian-Kindle-Books.com and ChristianWalk.net (winner of 8 prestigious awards). She shares a passion with her sister, Krystal Kuehn, in helping people live their best life now and reach their maximum potential. Violet has authored several best-selling books.
For a Complete List go to:
http://www.amazon.com/author/violetjames

LinkedIn: http://www.linkedin.com/in/violetjames

You can download *In Christ, I am...* in AUDIO version and listen on your Kindle™ tablet, iPhone®, iPod®, and Android™. Download it at Amazon.com or Audible.com or iTunes.

Your Free Gift

As a way of saying *thanks* for your purchase, we're offering this free must-have book that's exclusive to our readers.

7 Things to Do Every Day for a Prosperous Day
by Krystal Kuehn, MA, LPC, LLP, NCC

Live each new day with victory and joy!!

When you subscribe to our newsletter via email, you will get free, immediate access to download the ebook.

You can download this free ebook by going here:

www.ProsperousDay.com

14419312R00060

Printed in Poland
by Amazon Fulfillment
Poland Sp. z o.o., Wrocław